more Christmas with Style

Holiday Favorites
Arranged for the Piano
by Jerry Ray

Little did I know when I wrote *CHRISTMAS WITH STYLE* several years ago, that it would be so enthusiastically welcomed by beginning and advanced students and teachers alike. Your letters have indicated how you appreciate the simplicity of the arrangements and the full, rich harmonies achieved with such little effort.

I have always believed in the premise that a lot of great music can be made with just a few notes. And since those notes can be played by the beginning student as well as the seasoned veteran, every pianist is then capable of a truly outstanding musical performance.

I wrote the first book based on that ideal and have carried the same basic philosophy into this sequel. I have selected eight additional holiday favorites, a medley, and have added *Christmas with Style Overture* to bring you *MORE CHRISTMAS WITH STYLE.*

Now, go over and turn on the twinkling tree lights, throw a large log on the crackling fire, invite some friends over and sit down at the piano and give them the best gift of all—music. And a *CHRISTMAS WITH STYLE.*

Happy Holidays!

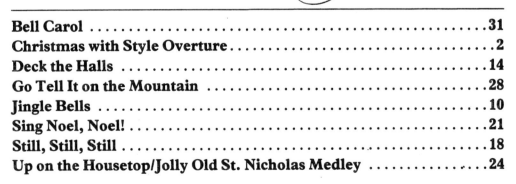

A high quality chrome cassette featuring Jerry Ray performing these arrangements is available for $7.95. Order #2533 from your favorite music store or contact:
Alfred Publishing Co., Inc.
16380 Roscoe Blvd., P.O. Box 10003
Van Nuys, CA 91410-0003

Art direction and design by Ted Engelbart, photo by Evan Wilcox. Special thanks to Mort and Iris Manus, Julia Fraser and Patrick Menders.

Christmas with Style Overture

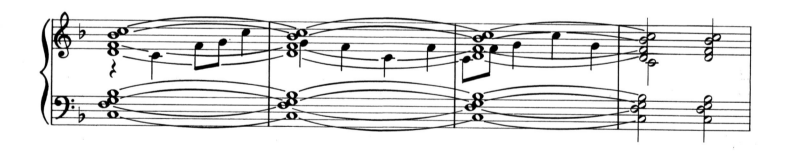

Jingle Bells
Not too fast—with a comical flair

4

*The low D in the right hand may be played in the left hand, and rolled, to accommodate the reach.

Deck the Halls
Brightly—with energy

6

Still, Still, Still
Moderately slow—with much expression

Sing Noel, Noel!
Expressively

8

Up on the Housetop
Not too fast

Jingle Bells

James Pierpont

Not too fast—with a comical flair

*The low D in the right hand may be played in the left hand, and rolled, to accommodate the reach.

Deck the Halls

Traditional

*Begin the trill very slowly, increasing tempo in a "comical" way.

Still, Still, Still

Traditional

Moderately slow—with much expression

Sing Noel, Noel!

Traditional

Up on the Housetop/Jolly Old St. Nicholas

Medley

Up on the Housetop: B. R. Hanby
Jolly Old St. Nicholas: Traditional

Not too fast

Go Tell It on the Mountain

Traditional

*The low F in the right hand may be played with the left, and rolled, to accommodate the reach.

Bell Carol

Traditional Ukrainian Carol